Identity Theft

Trends, Patterns, and Typologies Reported in Suspicious Activity Reports

Filed by Depository Institutions
January 1, 2003 – December 31, 2009

October 2010

Identity Theft

Trends, Patterns, and Typologies Reported in Suspicious Activity Reports

Filed by Depository Institutions
January 1, 2003 – December 31, 2009

October 2010

Table of Contents

INTRODUCTION

Identity theft is a crime rarely committed as an end in itself. Instead, identity theft is nearly always a means of facilitating another crime–usually a financial crime that enriches the perpetrator at the expense of individuals, businesses, financial institutions, or government agencies.

Reports of identity theft have been increasing for more than a decade. FinCEN highlighted this trend found in depository institution Suspicious Activity Report (SAR) filings as early as June 2001 in its semi-annual publication *The SAR Activity Review: Trends, Tips and Issues*.[1] The continuing upward trend in identity theft reporting prompted FinCEN to add identity theft as a characterization of suspicious activity on its depository institution SAR form (SAR) in July 2003 and on its securities and futures industries SAR form (SAR-SF) in May 2004.

Other federal agencies have also reported on identity theft. For example, in November 2007, the Federal Trade Commission (FTC) published the results of a study intended to gauge the impacts that identity theft has had on the general public.[2] In April 2007, The President's Identity Theft Task Force released a report on identity theft typologies and their scope, and on potential remedies to lessen the incidence of identity theft.[3] Subsequently, the U.S. Department of the Treasury, the federal banking agencies, and the FTC jointly issued Identity Theft Red Flag Reporting Rules for all businesses holding customer financial accounts potentially vulnerable to identity theft.[4] The rules went into effect on November 1, 2008.

---

1. See pages 14-17 at http://www.fincen.gov/news_room/rp/files/sar_tti_02.pdf

2. *Federal Trade Commission – Identity Theft Survey Report*, November 2007. Prepared by Synovate. See http://www.ftc.gov/bcp/edu/microsites/idtheft/ This study used data derived from a national telephone survey of several thousand randomly selected adults. This data collection methodology was chosen because individuals reporting identity theft to the FTC represent only an estimated 4 percent of all identity theft victims; generally only those who follow FTC guidelines to the letter. Consequently, the FTC did not believe that a sampling of this group would comprise a representative sample of all identity theft victims.

3. *Combating Identity Theft – A Strategic Plan, The President's Identity Theft Task Force*, April 2007. See http://www.idtheft.gov/

4. 16 CFR Part 681- Identity Theft Rules. Also see pages 40-44 of the October 2008 issue of *The SAR Activity Review – Trends, Tips & Issues* at http://www.fincen.gov/news_room/rp/files/sar_tti_14.pdf

Previous studies of identity theft have been based on survey responses. The FTC-commissioned study and other authoritative private industry identity theft studies relied upon data collected in scientifically-designed telephone surveys conducted with members of the general public. In contrast, this study is based upon the content of identity theft-related SAR filings submitted by depository institutions.[5]

---

5. Future FinCEN reports will describe trends and patterns in identity theft-related SARs filed by the securities and futures industry, by casinos, and by money services businesses.

EXECUTIVE SUMMARY

Identity theft was the sixth most frequently reported characterization of suspicious activity within the period of the study, behind structuring/money laundering, check fraud, mortgage loan fraud, credit card fraud, and counterfeit check fraud. Based upon analysis of the study sample, the number of identity theft-related depository institution SAR filings submitted during calendar year (CY) 2009 was 123 percent higher than the number reported in CY 2004. This compares with an 89 percent increase in the numbers of all depository institution SAR filings made in CY 2004 versus CY 2009.[6]

Over 86 percent of sample depository institution SAR filings bearing either the identity theft suspicious activity characterization or identity theft-associated keywords in their narratives actually described identity theft. Most of the remainder of the filings described identity fraud or provided insufficient information to confirm identity theft.[7]

Credit card fraud was the most frequently co-reported suspicious activity characterization with identity theft, appearing in over 45.5 percent of sample filings.[8] In about 30 percent of these filings reporting the successful takeover of an existing credit card account, and 17 percent reporting the successful unauthorized set up of a new credit card account, the alleged identity thief added his/her name to the account as an authorized user.

Several types of loan accounts were reportedly abused in 31 percent of filings. In 56.5 percent of filings specifically reporting student loan fraud, subjects included both their name and the victim's name on the loan application as either the borrower or co-signer.

---

6. The numbers of identity theft-characterized filings increased every year until 2009, when the number of filings fell by 9 percent. See the methodology section for the underlying numbers.

7. Most of the other filings marked as "identity theft" actually described identity fraud. Identity fraud differs from identity theft in that identity fraud involves the use of fabricated identifiers not tied to any true-named individual. Identity theft involves the use of identifying information unique to the rightful owner without the rightful owner's permission.

8. Each SAR filing may report several different characterizations of suspicious activity.

Analysis of the sample indicated that filers reporting auto loan fraud facilitated by identity theft were successful in identifying these loans as fraudulent prior to funding in 49.5 percent of filings. Similarly, filers reporting student loan fraud facilitated by identity theft identified the loans as fraudulent prior to funding in 54.5 percent of filings.

Nearly 27.5 percent of sample identity theft SAR narratives reported that the identity theft victim knew the suspected thief, who was usually a family member, friend, acquaintance, or an employee working in the victim's home. Computer-assisted identity theft was described in 4 percent of filings. Fraud rings that employ identity theft to further their illicit activities were reported in 3.5 percent of filings overall, with the year-to-year trend line strongly up in every period except 2005-2006.

Victims reportedly discovered identity theft through review of their own account activity in about 28 percent of filings in the sample. Filers credited routine financial institution account monitoring with uncovering identity theft in nearly another 21 percent of sample filings, and checks of commercial databases at account set-up in 14.5 percent of sample filings. Credit reports, law enforcement investigations, collection agencies, and credit monitoring services were responsible for revealing identity theft in a decreasing percentage of sample filings.

METHODOLOGY

For this study, FinCEN defined identity theft as using identifying information unique to the rightful owner without the rightful owner's permission. Unique identifying information includes financial account numbers, such as those used for depository accounts, investments, loans, credit cards, or online payment accounts; officially-issued federal or state identifying documents; and biometric information. An individual's use of another person's Social Security Number (SSN) or Taxpayer Identification Number (TIN) was considered identity theft regardless of whether the individual knew whether, or to whom, the number was issued. Additionally, impersonation of an actual person without consent was considered identity theft regardless of whether the impersonation occurred in person or through any other medium, electronic or otherwise.

FinCEN analysts conducted database research to identify SARs filed between January 1, 2003, and December 30, 2009, in which filers checked the box specifying identity theft as a characterization of suspicious activity. Analysts added a relatively small number of filings to the study population based on additional database searches, to identity SAR forms that lacked the identity theft characterization but contained one or more identity theft-associated key words in their narratives.

Findings were based upon the weighted combination of data results from two studies–the first analyzing a random sample of filings received between January 1, 2003, and September 30, 2008, and the second analyzing a random sample of filings received between October 1, 2008, and December 31, 2009.[9]

---

9. Weighting was determined based on the percentage of documents in each sample found to actually report identity theft multiplied by the number of filings initially determined to meet study parameters.

GENERAL STATISTICS

CY 2004 was the first full year in which depository institutions were obliged to report identity theft as a separate suspicious activity characterization on SARs. Since January 1, 2004, the number of SAR filings reporting identity theft has increased by 123 percent, from 16,051 in CY 2004 to 35,771 in CY 2009.[10] During the same period, the overall incidence of SAR filings increased 89 percent, from 380,975 in CY 2004 to 720,309 in CY 2009   Graph 1 displays the annual filing numbers of SAR forms bearing the identity theft suspicious activity characterization.[11]

GRAPH 1

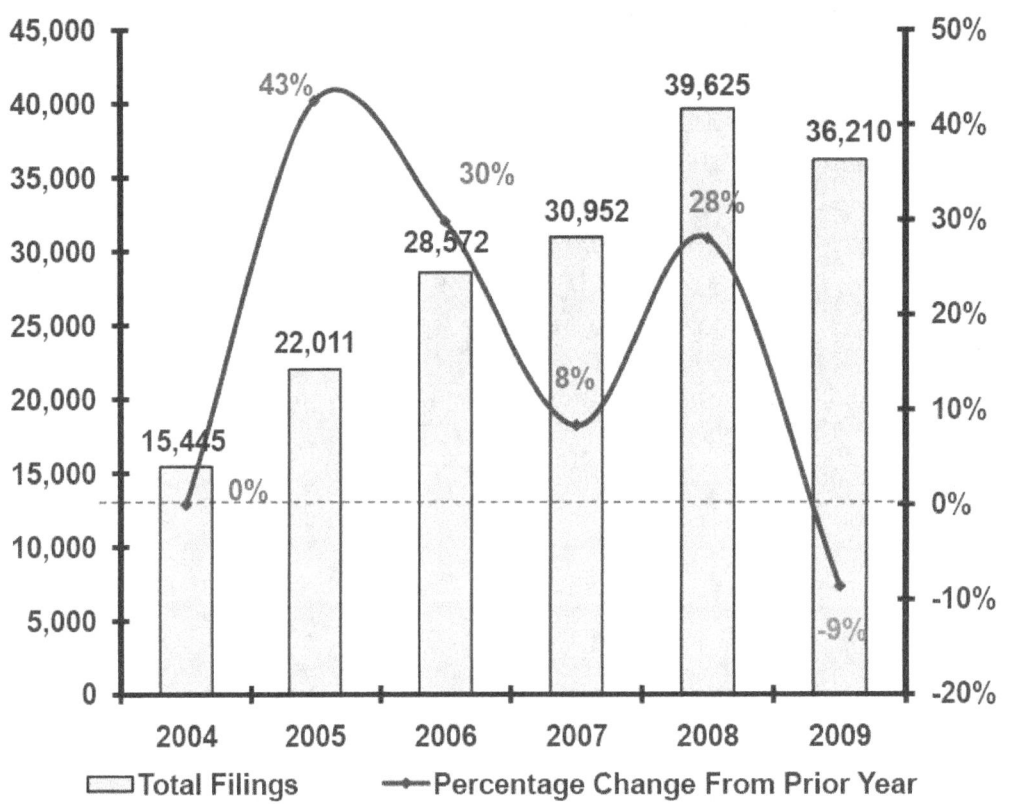

□ Total Filings   **━━ Percentage Change From Prior Year**

---

10. These numbers were calculated by multiplying the number of filings identified using the specific me hodology by the percen age of the analyzed sample by year found to actually describe identity theft.

11. The identity theft suspicious activity characterization first appeared on the SAR form in 2003. Since the form did not bear this characterization until the middle of the year, FinCEN omitted 2003 data from **Graph 1** [*edited November 9, 2010*]

The year-on-year percentage increases in identity theft-characterized filings were high in the first years after identity theft became a separate characterization in 2003, but fell off significantly by 2007. The rebound noted in 2008 may have related to heightened filer awareness and attention precipitated by the identity theft red flag reporting requirements that went into effect on November 1, 2008. The absolute number of identity theft-characterized filings fell in 2009, as did the number of all depository institution filings, albeit by less than 2 percent.

Based on the sampled SARs, 373 different institutions filed reports of identity theft. As shown in **Chart 1**, the top 10 filers were responsible for just over half the filings.

CHART 1

Top Ten Identity Theft Depository Institution Filer Concentration

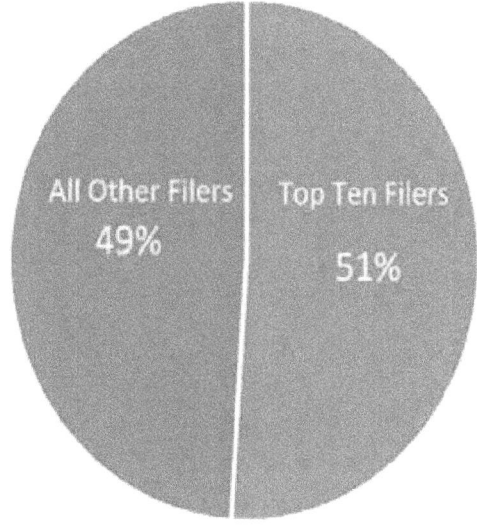

TYPOLOGIES, TRENDS & PATTERNS

Sample filings reported three main types of fraud facilitated by identity theft: credit card fraud, all types of loan fraud, and depository account fraud. As noted in **Graph 2** and **Graph 3**, the data shows a shift away from identity theft to facilitate credit card fraud and toward identity theft to facilitate mortgage loan fraud and all types of consumer loan fraud, especially auto and student loan fraud.

GRAPH 2

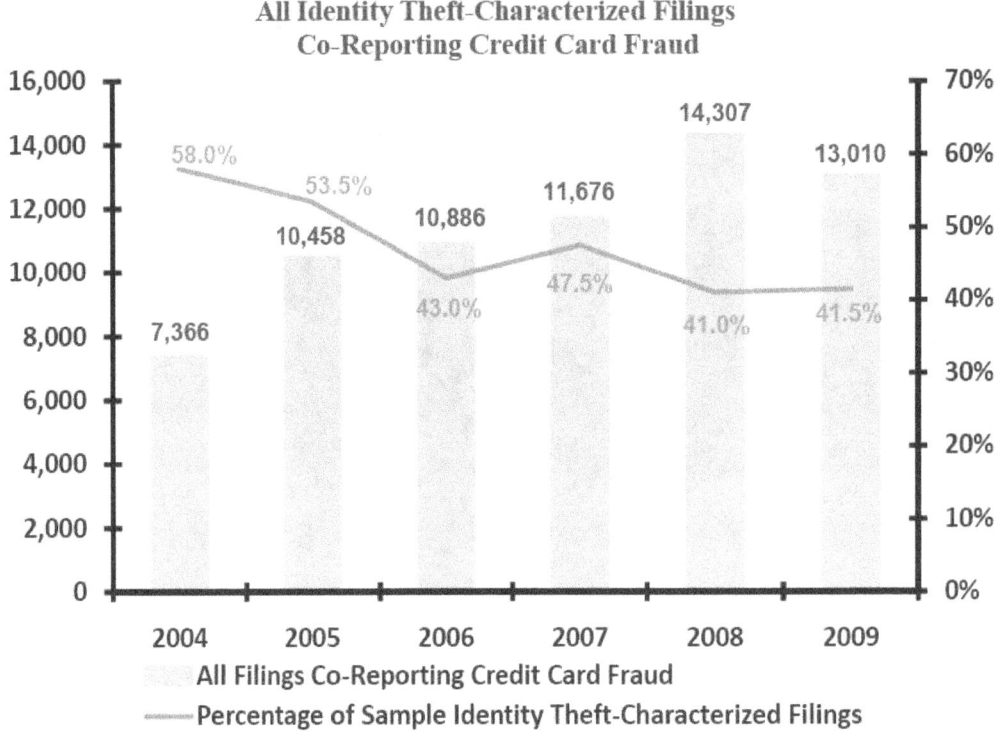

**All Identity Theft-Characterized Filings
Co-Reporting Credit Card Fraud**

All Filings Co-Reporting Credit Card Fraud

Percentage of Sample Identity Theft-Characterized Filings

As can be seen in **Graph 2**, though the absolute number of co-reported credit card filings continued to rise until 2009, the rate of increase did not keep pace with increases in identity theft-characterized filings during most of the 2004-2009 period.

GRAPH 3

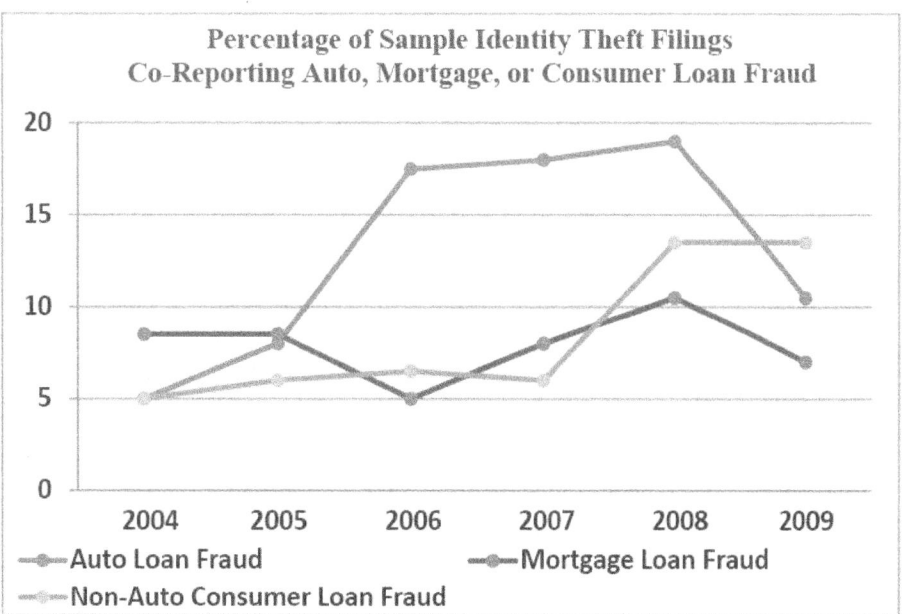

Credit Card Fraud

Credit card fraud was the most prevalent type of identity theft-facilitated fraud reported during the study period. Identity thieves reportedly engineered takeovers of existing legitimate credit card accounts and set up new unauthorized accounts using the identifying information of identity theft victims Reports often described physical theft of credit cards from the mail or from the person or residence of the victim.

Cards also were reportedly stolen by virtual means through the skimming of credit card numbers in the course of normal commerce; or through collection of this information online as a result of personal computer viral infection or consumer response to phishing emails and spoofed Web sites [12] In some cases, suspects used stolen credit card numbers to create a usable copy of the credit card (a cloned card). Individuals often reportedly used stolen credit card numbers without having physical custody of the card in non-point-of-sale transactions conducted over the Internet, by phone, or by mail.

---

12. Skimming is the process by which the identity thief collects credit card information when the card is presented or the credit card number is provided in any sales transaction. Skimming most frequently refers to the electronic collection of credit card information using an instrument made for this purpose, but may also involve simple manual collection.

Graph 4 displays the percentage of sample filings by year reporting each type of credit card account-related abuse facilitated by identity theft. Credit card fraud was co-reported in about 45.5 percent of the sample SAR filings.

GRAPH 4

Percentage of Sample SAR Filings Reporting Noted Types of Credit Card Account Abuse Facilitated by Identity Theft

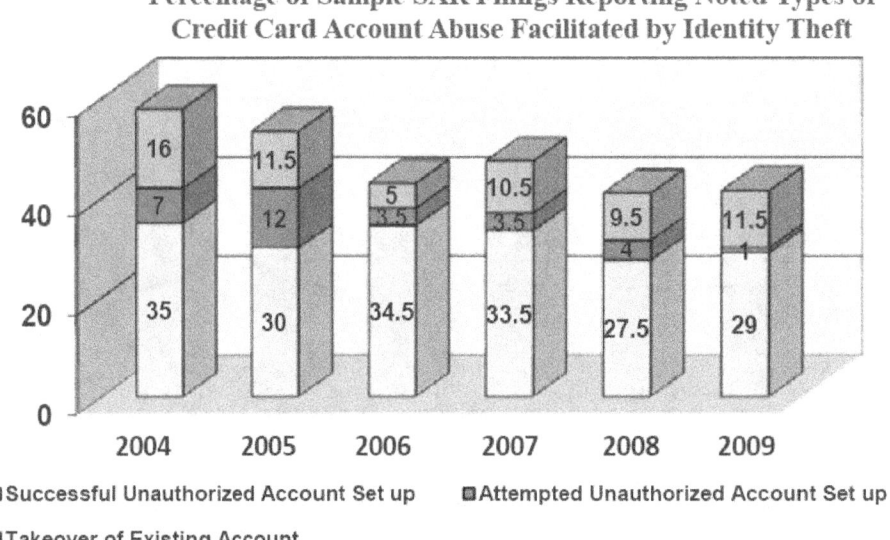

☐ Successful Unauthorized Account Set up   ☐ Attempted Unauthorized Account Set up

☐ Takeover of Existing Account

Graph 4 illustrates that the percentage of sample filings reporting credit card fraud as a co-reported suspicious activity characterization with identity theft declined between 2004 and 2006 and reached a plateau thereafter.

Attempts to Become Authorized Purchasers

Interestingly, in over 30 percent of sample filings that reported the takeover of an existing legitimate credit card account, the subject reportedly added his/her own name as an authorized user of the card Likewise, in almost 17 percent of sample filings reporting the successful set-up of one or more unauthorized credit card accounts using victim identifiers, the subject included his/her name as an authorized purchaser along with the victim

It would seem counterintuitive that identity thieves would connect their actual names to accounts they abuse for fear of giving away their identity in any ensuing investigation. However, in 15.5 percent of sample filings in which identity thieves reportedly added their names to legitimate existing accounts, and in 44.5 percent of sample filings in which they reportedly included their names as authorized purchasers on unauthorized new accounts set-up using victim identifiers, the suspected thieves were family members, friends, or, in several cases, employees of the victim.[13]

Individuals not known to the victims who reportedly added names to legitimate accounts apparently did so for ease of use. However, the names added were often fraudulent or were names of other true-named persons for whom the thieves possessed credible identification.

Private Label Cards

Of the sample filings that described attempted or successful unauthorized credit card account set-up, nearly 11.5 percent reported private label ("store") card account set-ups.[14] All but a few of these filings (97 percent) reported the account set-up as successful.[15] This compares with an overall successful set-up rate estimated from the sample of about 88 percent. The significantly higher success rate in setting up unauthorized private label card accounts may relate to the "instant credit" offered by many retailers that issue private label cards. Issuers not only allow but often incentivize the use of these cards beginning on the day the application is completed at the issuing retail establishment.

Accounts Opened under Business Names

In about 8 percent of sample filings, the reported identity thief set up unauthorized new accounts in the name of a business, listing a principal of the business as the payment guarantor.

---

13. In practice, many retail establishments make no apparent effort to identify credit card users, relying largely instead on automatic authorization systems in place to alert the sales clerk to flagged or blocked credit card accounts. Many systems in use today also flag cards showing usage patterns inconsistent with prior patterns recorded for the particular account. Though this software can be helpful in identifying accounts that have been taken over without the legitimate account holder's knowledge, they may be of little help in identifying new, unauthorized accounts.

14. Private label cards are "store cards" issued bearing the name of a retailer. Many are processed through one of the major card networks (mainly Visa or MasterCard) and bear that logo as well. Others are issued and processed completely in-store. All private label cards share certain characteristics, including that they may only be used at the issuing business and do not allow balance transfers or cash withdrawals. See http://www.nytimes.com/2009/02/10/your-money/credit-and-debit-cards/10private.html.

15. A successful setup is defined as one in which the card is issued to the identity thief and used to secure merchandise.

Loan Fraud

About 31 percent of sample SAR filings reported successful and unsuccessful attempts at loan fraud, including fraud related to loans for automobiles, mortgages, student loans, and other types of consumer loans.

Auto Loan Fraud

The percentage of sample SAR filings reporting attempts to use identity theft to facilitate auto loan fraud was about twice as high as for other type of loans until 2009. As **Graph 5** shows, reporting on auto loan fraud facilitated by identity theft increased rapidly from 2004-2006 as a percentage of all sample identity theft filings, then increased at a much slower rate through 2008, and fell in 2009. About 10.5 percent of the identity theft-associated sample SARs filed in 2009 reported successful or attempted auto loan fraud.

GRAPH 5

Percentage of Sample SAR Filings Reporting Successful & Attempted Auto Loan Fraud Facilitated by Identity Theft

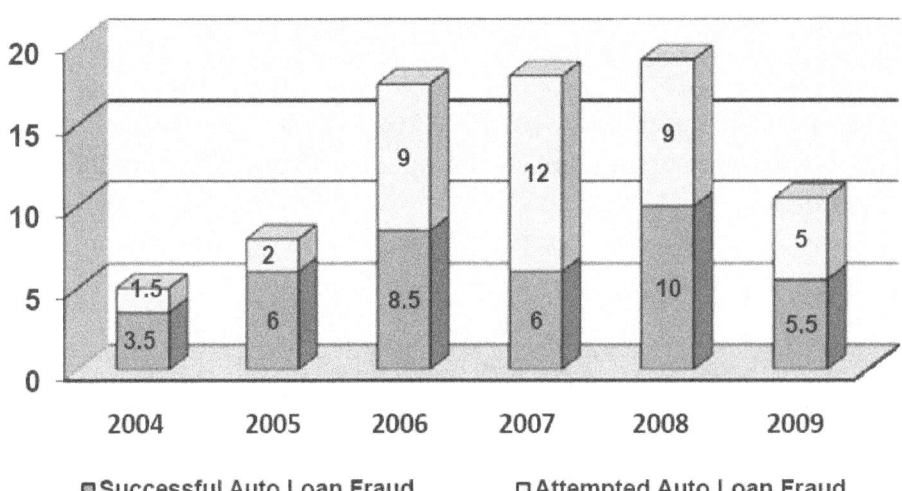

■Successful Auto Loan Fraud   □Attempted Auto Loan Fraud

The data suggest that filers making auto loans have had significant success in identifying such fraudulent loans before they are funded. Overall, slightly less than 50 percent of the fraudulent auto loans reported in the sample data were detected prior to funding.

Mortgage Loan Fraud

As shown in **Graph 6**, filing trends indicate that identity theft-facilitated mortgage loan fraud reporting was up through 2008, but fell in 2009. The sample data show a downward reporting trend in the percentage of such loans identified prior to funding. This trend may result from increased filer scrutiny and awareness of the factors contributing to foreclosure rather than to an actual increase in successful identity theft-associated mortgage loan fraud. Data from a recent mortgage loan fraud quarterly update indicates that the majority of mortgage loan fraud-associated SAR filings submitted recently reference mortgages granted more than 2 years prior to the SAR submission date.[16]

GRAPH 6

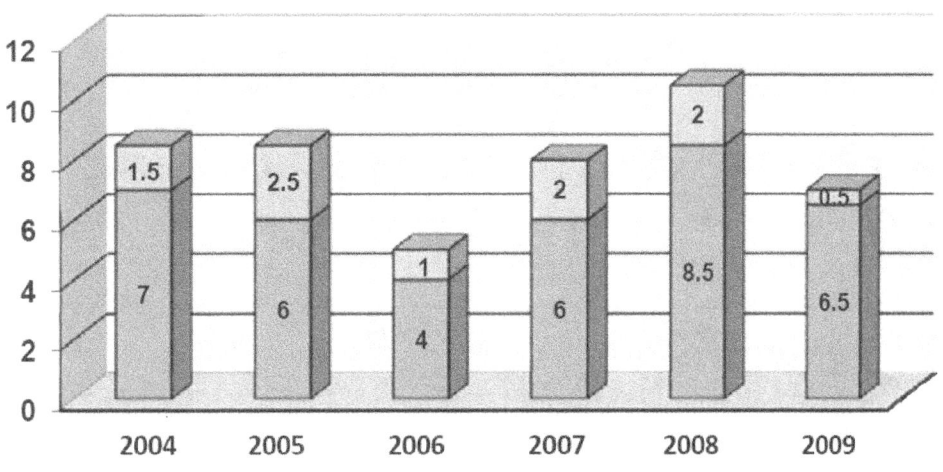

Percentage of Sample SAR Filings Reporting Successful & Attempted Mortgage Loan Fraud Facilitated by Identity Theft

□ Attempted Mortgage Loan Fraud   ▨ Successful Mortgage Loan Fraud

Through 2008, only 0.35 percent of sample filings reported the successful takeover of home equity line of credit accounts (HELOCs). Conversely, nearly 2 percent of sample 2009 identity theft-associated filings referenced the abuse or attempted abuse of HELOCs.

---

16. See http://www.fincen.gov/news_room/rp/files/MLF_Update.pdf

Consumer Loan Fraud

Beginning in 2006, student loan fraud accounted for the largest plurality of identity theft facilitated non-auto consumer loan fraud sample reports, representing 46.5 percent of all such sample filings during the 2006-2009 study periods. The consumer loan fraud sample data indicate an overall shift away from auto and mortgage loan fraud, toward student loan fraud. The success rate noted in the sample in identifying such loans prior to funding has varied year-by-year. Overall, 54.5 percent of fraudulent student loans reported in the sample were detected prior to funding.

In over 56.5 percent of the sample filings reporting attempted or successful student loan fraud, the alleged identity thief listed both the victim and himself/herself on the loan as recipient or co-signer. **Graph 7** displays sample data from filings that reported consumer loan fraud not related to mortgage or auto loans.

GRAPH 7

Percentage of Sample SAR Filings Reporting Successful & Attempted Consumer Loan Fraud Facilitated by Identity Theft

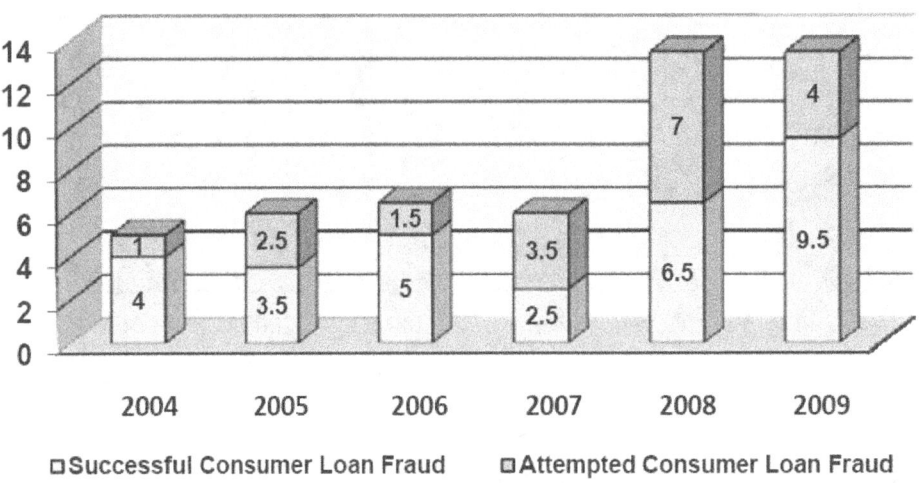

☐Successful Consumer Loan Fraud   ☐Attempted Consumer Loan Fraud

Depository Account Fraud

Though not a characterization of suspicious activity appearing on SAR forms, analysis of the SAR sample noted a significant amount of abuse associated with depository accounts facilitated by identity theft as displayed in **Graph 8**.[17]

GRAPH 8

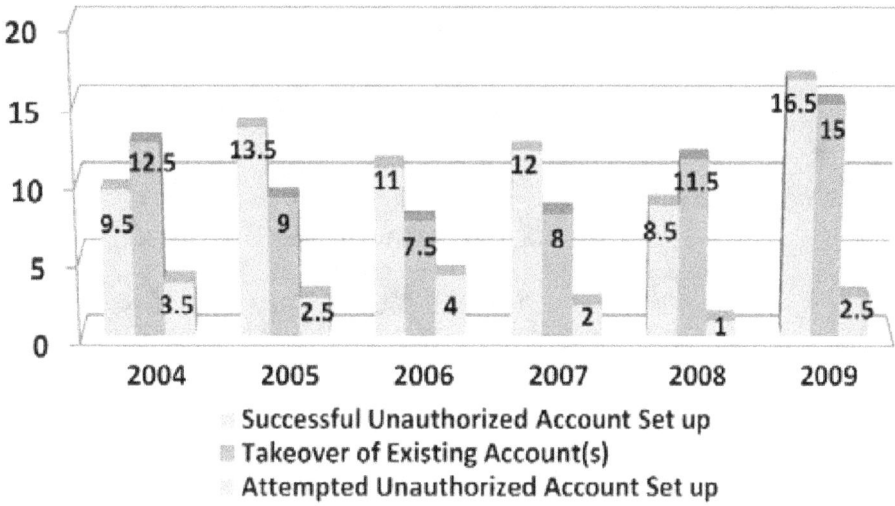

Percentage of Sample SAR Filings Reporting Noted Types of Depository Account Abuse Facilitated by Identity Theft

- Successful Unauthorized Account Set up
- Takeover of Existing Account(s)
- Attempted Unauthorized Account Set up

Though no trends are evident in the sample data by specific type of activity, the overall trend in reporting of depository account abuse facilitated by identity theft, measured as a percentage of total sample filings, was mildly down over the course of the study, but showed a rebound in 2009.

Akin to an identity thief who adds his/her name to an existing or new unauthorized credit or loan account, a frequently reported means of facilitation associated with depository accounts involves the identity thief who opens a new joint account in the name of the victim and him/herself. The identity thief then poses as the victim and directs that funds be transferred from one or more legitimate existing victim accounts into the new joint account, thus making these funds available to the identity thief.

---

17. Results are not stacked because a significant number of SAR narratives report both attempted and successful new account setups and/or account takeovers within the same SAR document. [*edited November 9, 2010*]

Application of the percentages reported in **Graph 8** to the total number of identity theft filings reported in **Graph 1** yields **Graph 9**.

GRAPH 9

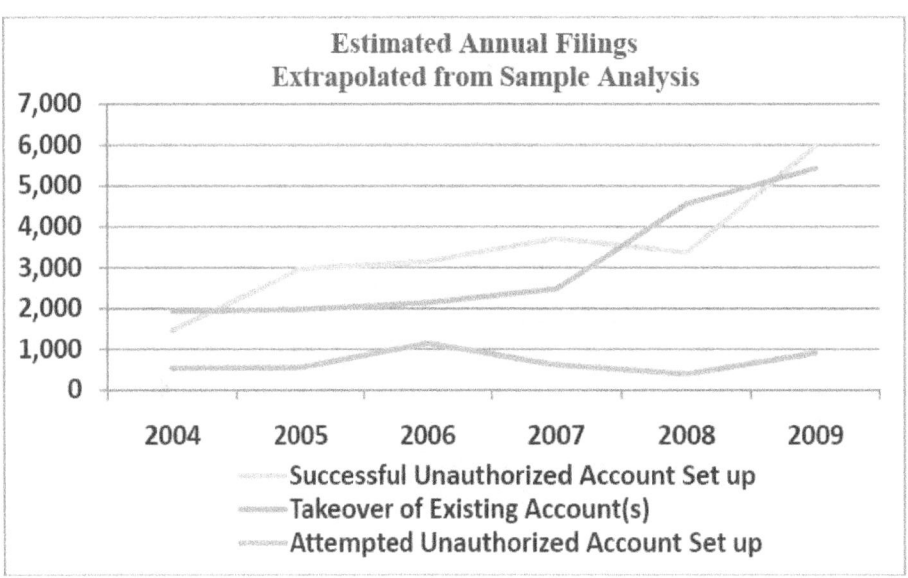

Graph 9 indicates that in terms of depository account abuse associated with identity theft, filers most frequently reported the successful set up of one or more unauthorized account(s) using victim identifiers (prevalently reported in 2005-2007 and 2009); followed by the takeover of one or more existing victim account(s) (prevalently reported in 2004 and 2008).[18]

Prepaid Cards and Probable Tax Refund Fraud

Overall, filers referenced prepaid cards in about one percent of the sample filings, submitted almost exclusively in 2008 and 2009. In all instances filers reported the set-up of multiple prepaid card accounts in different names using valid SSNs for each of the supplied names. The filers sent multiple cards in different names to the same address. Filers confirmed through commercial database searches that the mail-to addresses did not correspond with reported addresses for any of the relevant cardholders. Shortly after card activation, the filers received one or more ACH credit(s) from the U S. Treasury or from a state revenue office representing a

---

18. Numbers were derived by multiplying the annual percentages reported in Graph 8 by the corresponding annual numbers reported in Graph 1.

tax refund for the benefit of the cardholder.[19] Filers noted that the presumed identity thieves quickly drained card balances, mainly through ATM cash withdrawals, but sometimes also through point-of-sale (POS) merchandise purchases. When a filer's anti-money laundering software flagged such cards for abnormal activity on cards receiving loads above pre-determined levels, the filer reportedly blocked the card. Filer attempts to have the cardholder verify his/her identity were fruitless. [20]

Fraud and Identity Theft Rings

Somewhat less than 3.5 percent of sample filings reported the operation of known identity theft and/or fraud rings. Just over half reported that the filer had notified local, state, or federal law enforcement about these rings.

Table 1 shows the results of a search of all SARs reporting an identity theft characterization received between 2004 and 2009 that referenced a ring or conspiracy in the narrative section.

TABLE 1

Year	All SAR Filings Bearing an Identity Theft Characterization	All Identity Theft Filings with "Ring" or "Conspiracy" in Narrative	Percentage	Year-on-Year Percent Change
2004	15,445	284	1.84%	0%
2005	22,011	693	3.15%	71%
2006	28,572	806	2.82%	-10%
2007	30,952	1,017	3.29%	17%
2008	39,625	1,525	3.85%	17%
2009	36,210	2,170	5.99%	56%
TOTAL	172,815	6,495	3.76%	

As can be seen in Table 1, the proportional reporting trend for filings reporting both identity theft and the involvement of rings or conspiracies is steeply up, with the percentage of such filings increasing year-to-year in every period except 2005-2006.

---

19. These refunds were presumably the result of fraudulently submitted tax filings made using the valid names and identifying numbers of identity theft victims.

20. The prepaid cards used were invariably reloadable open-loop cards that allowed loads of at least $5,000. One of the most frequently reported cards employed was specifically issued to receive tax refunds.

Abuse of Employee and Customer Database Information

Twelve sample filings reported breaches of employee or customer databases.[21]   Filers reported that in four of these filings, a current or former employee was determined responsible for intentional breaches in order to sell identifying information to identity thieves. In 16 sample reports, filers said their own employees used customer information to defraud the filer. Another 10 sample filings reported employees setting up unauthorized accounts using customer identifiers so that the employee could meet sales or incentive goals. Filers reported mortgage loan professionals in six sample filings, auto dealership employees in three, and tax preparers in two. These individuals apparently abused customer-supplied identifiers to set up unauthorized credit, loan, or depository accounts.

Geographical Data

Most of the subjects named in the total population of 2009 identity theft-characterized SARs lived in states with the largest populations. **Table 2** lists the 2009 top 10 states in terms of distinct identity theft SAR subjects per state by zip code. Minnesota (7th), which ranks 21st by population, is a notable exception.

TABLE 2

Rank	State	2009 SAR Identity Theft Subjects by Subject Residence Zip Code
1	California	5,366
2	Florida	2,582
3	Texas	2,022
4	New York	1,931
5	Illinois	1,551
6	Georgia	1,402
7	Minnesota	1,031
8	Washington	1,005
9	Michigan	972
10	Pennsylvania	776

21. For purposes of the study, "breach" was narrowly defined to mean the compromise of sensitive customer/employee identifying information to individuals outside the company/organization legitimately retaining the data. Employee abuse of such data not involving compromise of the data to outside individuals was not considered a breach.

However, when the data is viewed proportionally, based on 2009 SAR identity theft subjects per 100,000 state residents, disproportionately high numbers of subjects surface in Minnesota (1st), Nevada (2nd), Utah (4th), Wisconsin (8th), and Kansas (9th), as noted in **Map 1**. The map shows the proportional incidence of identity theft subjects by subject residence zip code reported in all SAR filings received during the CY 2009, bearing an identity theft suspicious activity characterization.[22]

MAP 1

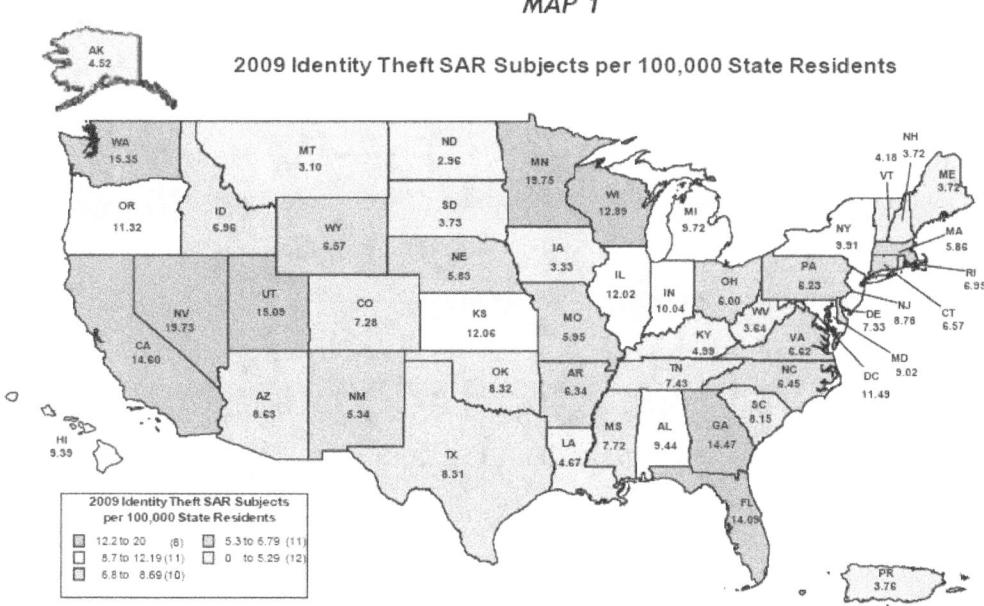

Fourteen states exceeded the average of 9 83 subjects per 100,000 state residents. The median was 7 33 subjects per 100,000 state residents.

Analysis using the same subject-based parameters employed to produce the map showed credit card fraud as the predominant co-reported characterization in most states during all reporting periods. However, several states showed notable variation. For example, **Graph 10** shows that a plurality of SAR-reported Wisconsin identity theft subjects were associated with mortgage loan fraud until 2009, when a plurality was instead reported to be associated with consumer loan fraud.

---

22. Numbers represent the proportional incidence of subjects reported per 100,000 state residents for CY 2009, in SARs bearing an identity theft suspicious activity characterization. Same subjects duplicated in the same zip code were deleted. Same subjects reported in multiple zip codes were retained. Though this methodology inflates the actual number of distinct subjects tied to multiple addresses in differing zip codes, it also provides a clearer indication of likely physical locations of identity theft perpetration. Research identified 30,268 distinct identity theft SAR subjects based on their reported residential zip codes. Research identified another 431 subjects that could be tied to a state, but not to a specific zip code. Both of these groups were included in the data to support Map 1. Another 3,596 reported subjects could not be tied to a specific state of residence. Data for these subjects was omitted from Map 1. Of these omitted subjects, 250 were tied to foreign residences.

GRAPH 10

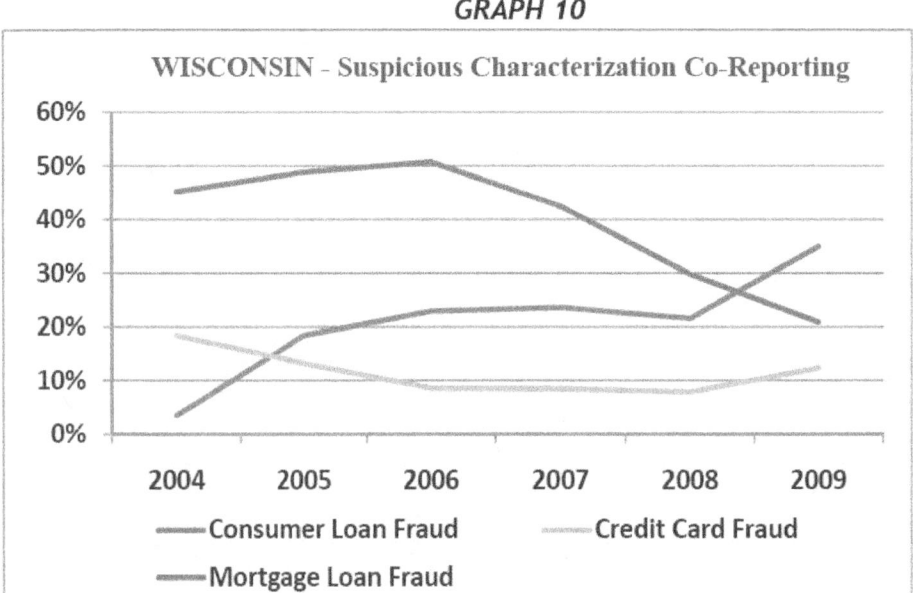

Graph 11 displays the absolute numbers of unique Wisconsin subjects reported by year associated with identity theft overall and with the specified co-reported suspicious activity characterizations. Notice that although the highest co-reporting percentage for mortgage loan fraud occurred in 2006, the greatest number of unique mortgage loan fraud subjects was reported in 2007, as the overall number of identity theft subjects increased markedly over 2006.

GRAPH 11

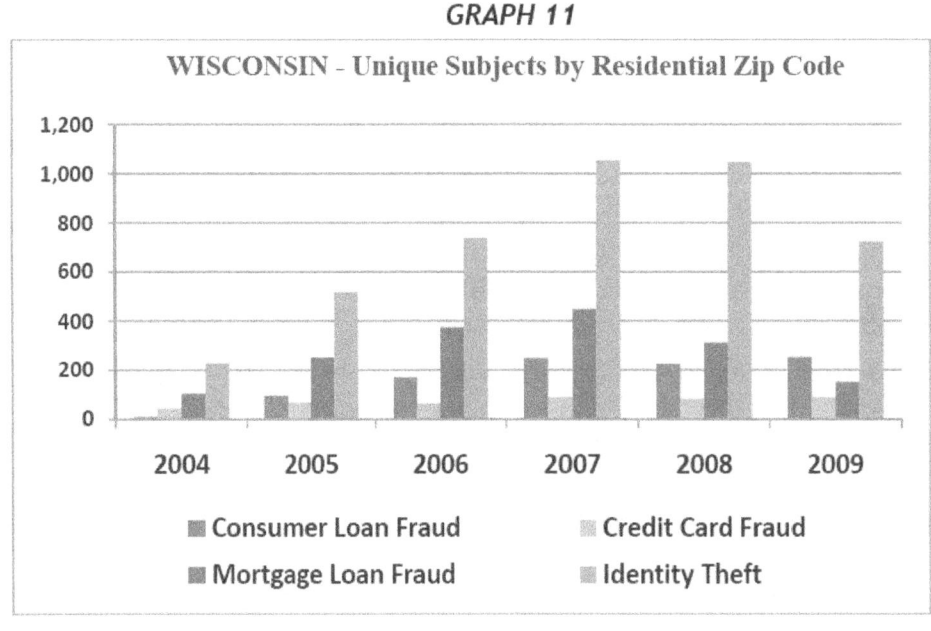

In Minnesota (**Graph 12**) by CY 2006 the number of identity theft subjects reportedly engaged in mortgage loan fraud surpassed the number engaged in credit card fraud. Mortgage loan fraud was a co-reported characterization associated with over 80 percent of identity theft subjects with a Minnesota address by 2008, before declining to 63 percent in 2009. [*edited November 9, 2010*]

GRAPH 12

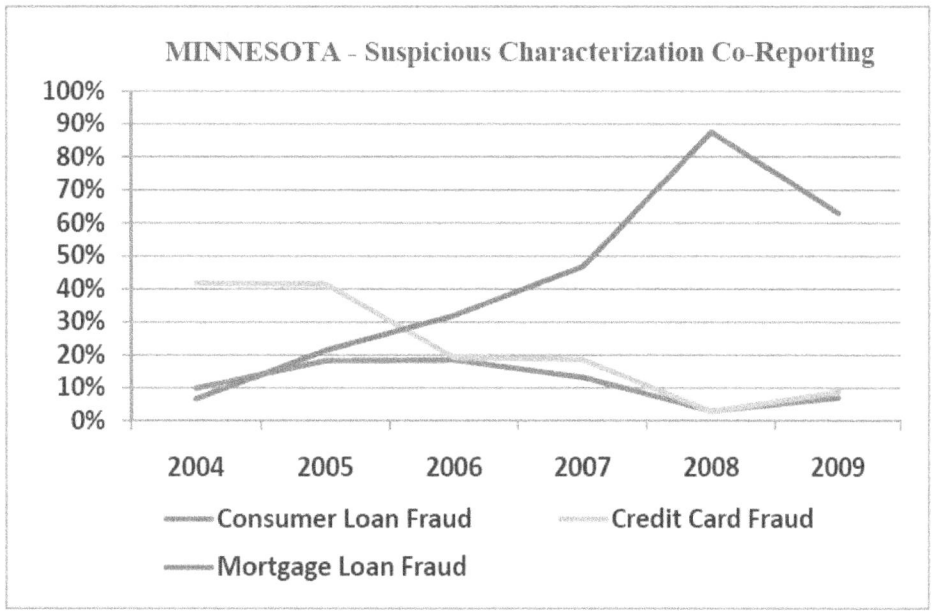

Graph 13 highlights the dramatic surge in 2008 of Minnesota identity theft subjects reportedly engaged almost exclusively in mortgage loan fraud and the subsequent decline reported in 2009.

GRAPH 13

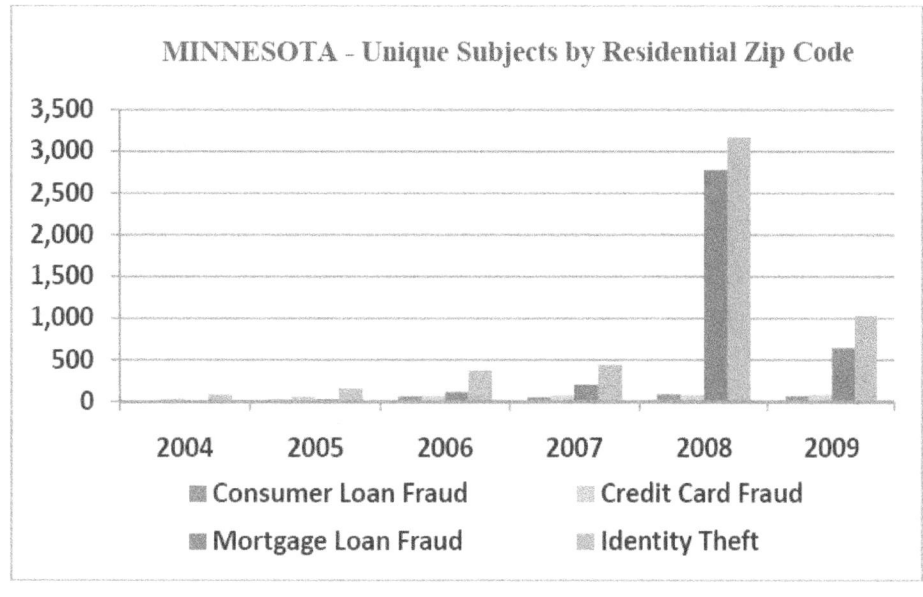

In Indiana (**Graph 14**), the number of identity theft subjects thought to be involved in mortgage loan fraud increased substantially after 2007, crossing a plummeting credit card fraud trend line in 2008.

GRAPH 14

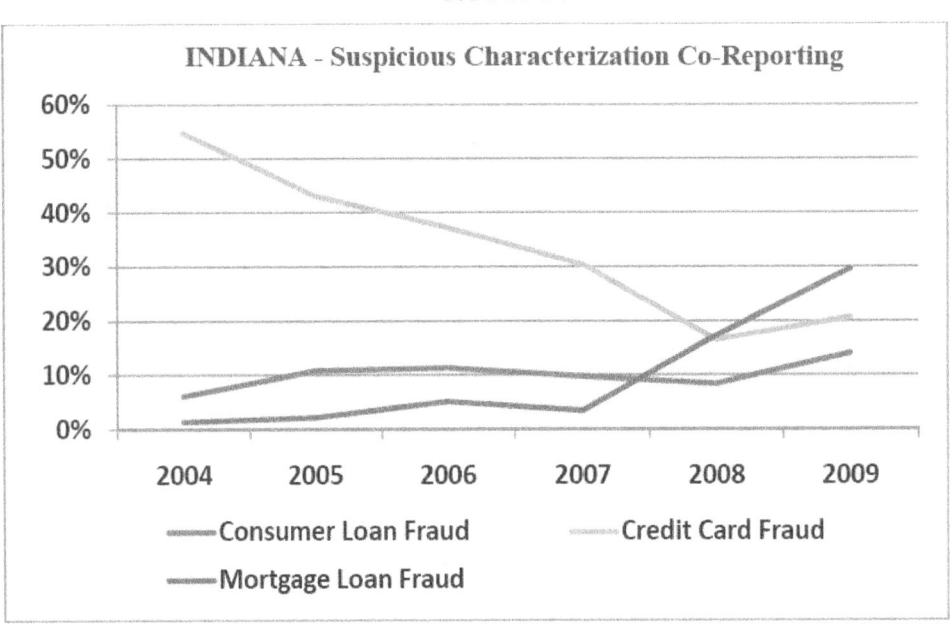

Graph 15 indicates the total number of unique Indiana identity theft subjects increased rapidly beginning in 2004, doubled in 2008 from its 2007 level (851 versus 411), before settling back to 628 in 2009.

GRAPH 15

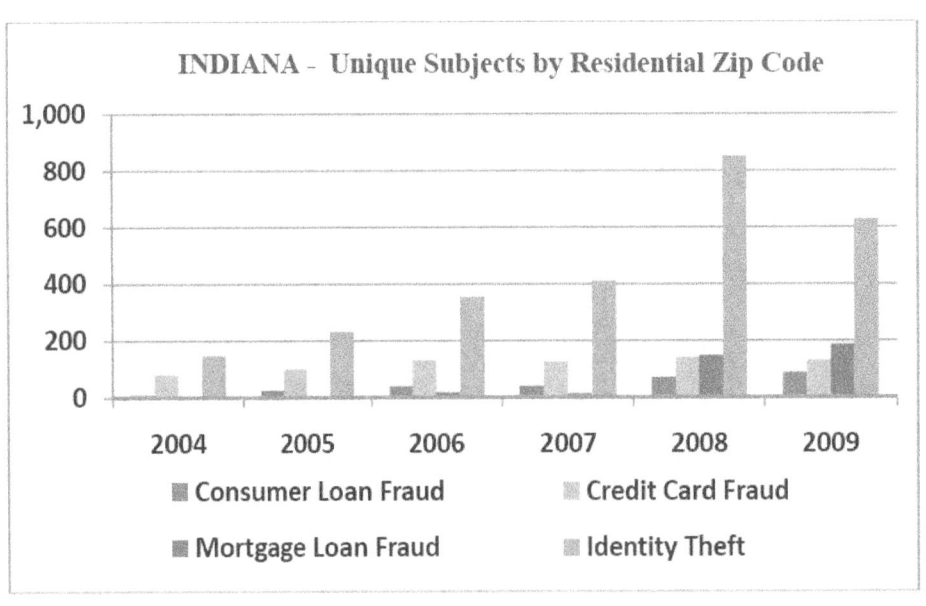

Washington (**Graph 16**), Utah (**Graph 18**), and Oregon (**Graph 20**) show similarly dramatic trend lines evidencing the predominance of identity theft subjects reportedly engaged in consumer loan fraud.

GRAPH 16

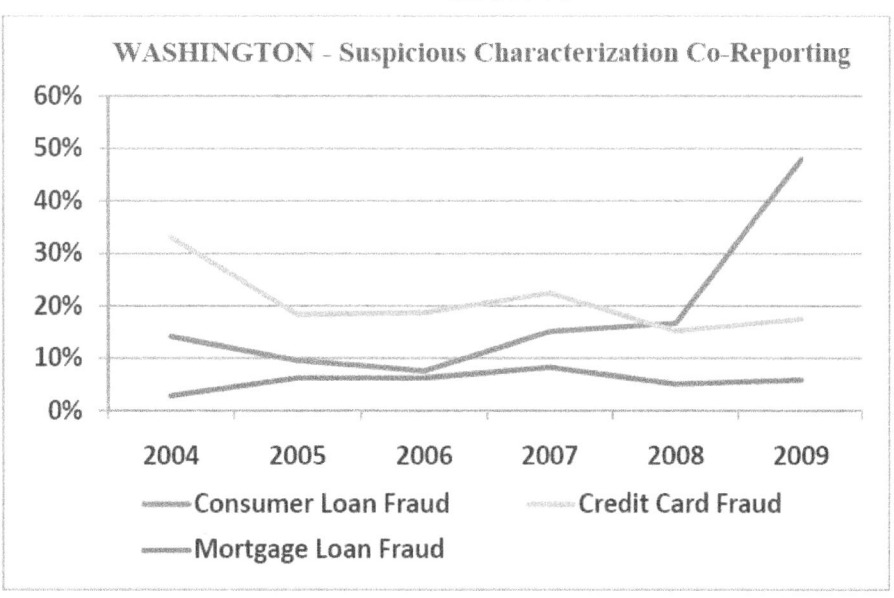

GRAPH 17

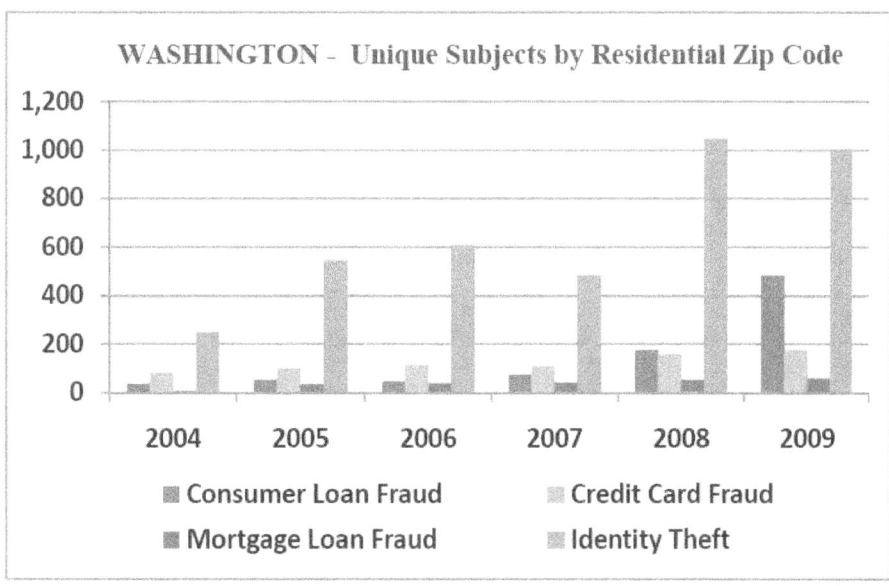

The number of Utah (**Graph 18**) identity theft subjects engaged in consumer loan fraud outstripped those engaged in credit card fraud by 2007.

GRAPH 18

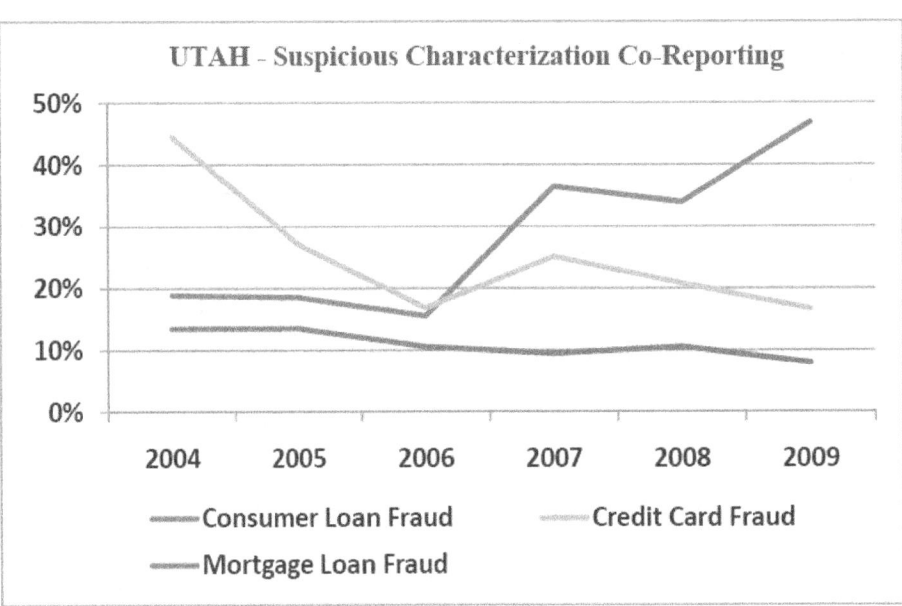

Note in **Graph 19** the persistent increase in the number of Utah identity theft subjects involved in consumer loan fraud   Interestingly, the increase does not appear to be strongly tied to the overall number of identity theft subjects, as can be seen in the 2007 figures.

GRAPH 19

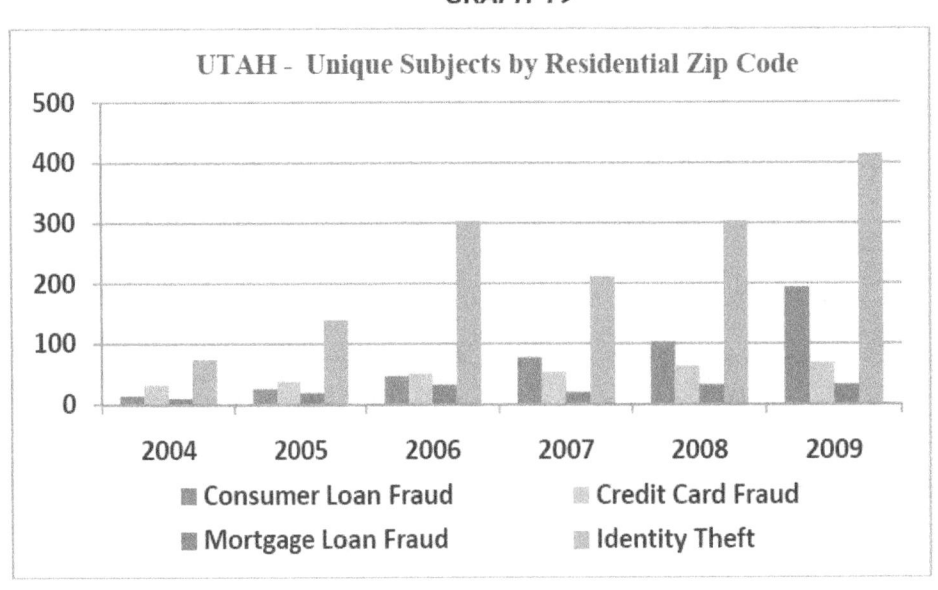

Oregon identity theft subjects (**Graph 20**) showed the earliest and most sustained penchant for involvement in consumer loan fraud, beginning in 2005.

GRAPH 20

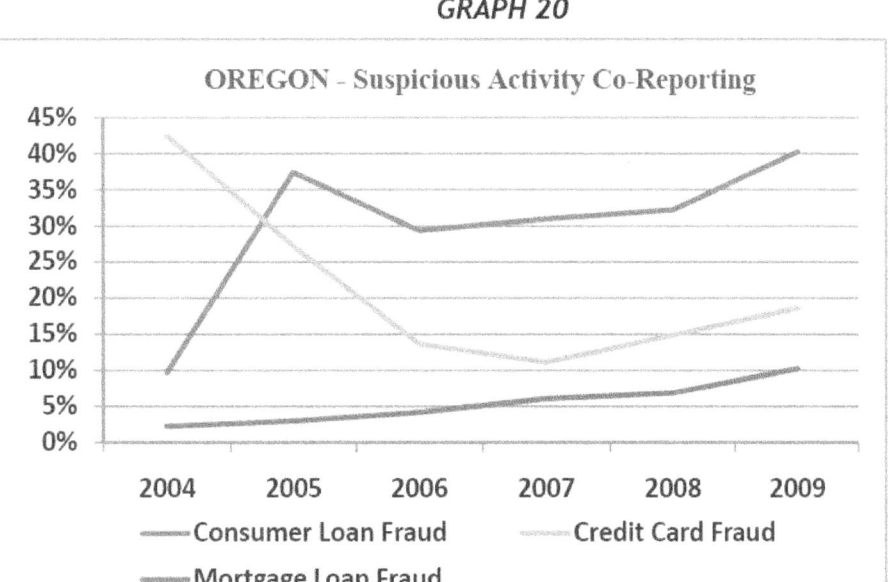

Graph 21 recounts the steady increase in Oregon identity theft subjects reportedly associated with consumer loan fraud.

GRAPH 21

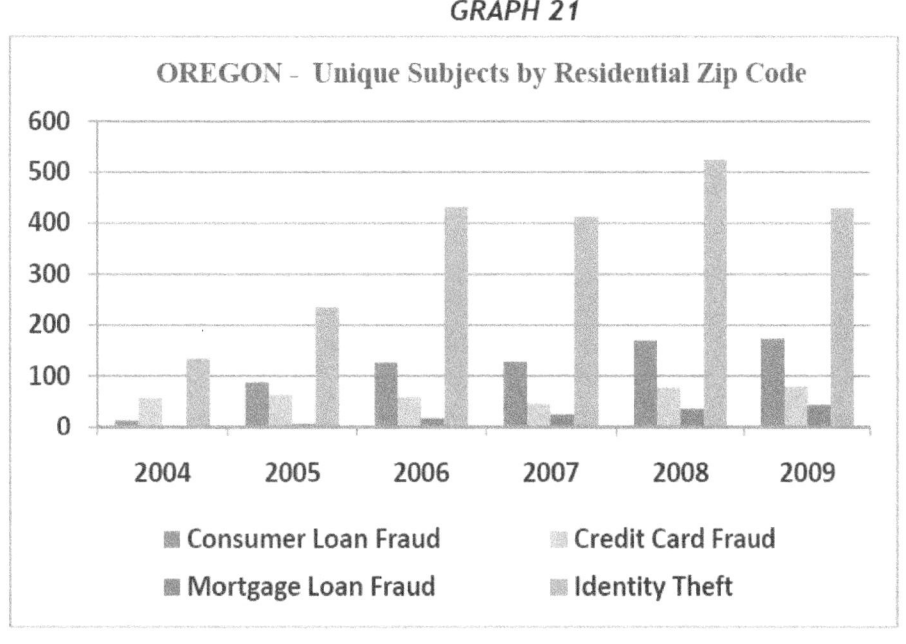

Nationally (**Graph 22**), SARs continue to report a plurality of identity theft subjects committing credit card fraud, though the trend line is consistently and moderately downwards. The trend line representing identity theft subjects involved in mortgage loan fraud was significantly up until a large decline in 2008-2009. The overall trend line in numbers of identity theft subjects associated with consumer loan fraud has been modestly but consistently up.

GRAPH 22[23]

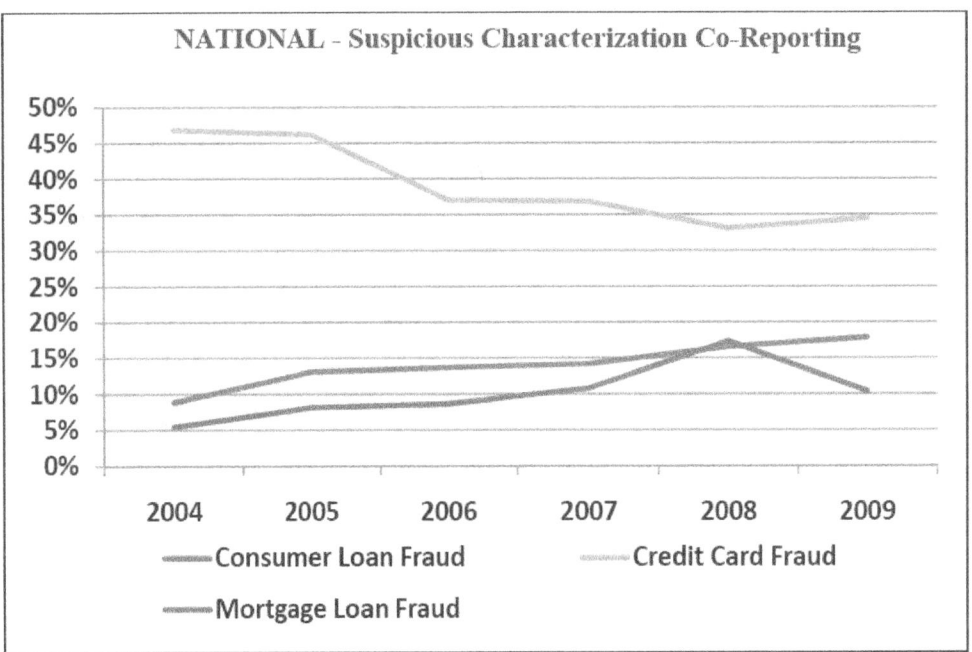

23. Although overall trend lines appearing in Graph 22 generally show the same general patterns as those noted in Graphs 2 and 3, percentages are significantly different. The data supporting Graphs 2 and 3 were derived from an analysis of sample filings. All sample filings were accorded equal weight regardless of the number of identified subjects per filing, to include filings identifying no subjects. Conversely, data supporting Graph 22 are subject-based, and were derived from a statistical summarization of all filings reporting an identity theft characterization. Filings were proportionally weighted based upon the number of reported subjects, delimited by the same parameters used for Map 1 (see footnote 22). Consequently, filings reporting no subjects were not included in the data supporting Graph 22.

A comparison of the overall numbers of unique identity theft subjects reported in **Graph 23** with the overall numbers of identity theft filings reported in **Graph 1** will demonstrate that the number of identity theft filings made from 2004 through 2009 exceeded the number of unique identity theft subject names reported during this period. In fact, of the 172,815 SAR filings characterized as identity theft during the 2004-2009 period, 49,715 (nearly 29 percent) reported no subject names at all.

GRAPH 23[24]

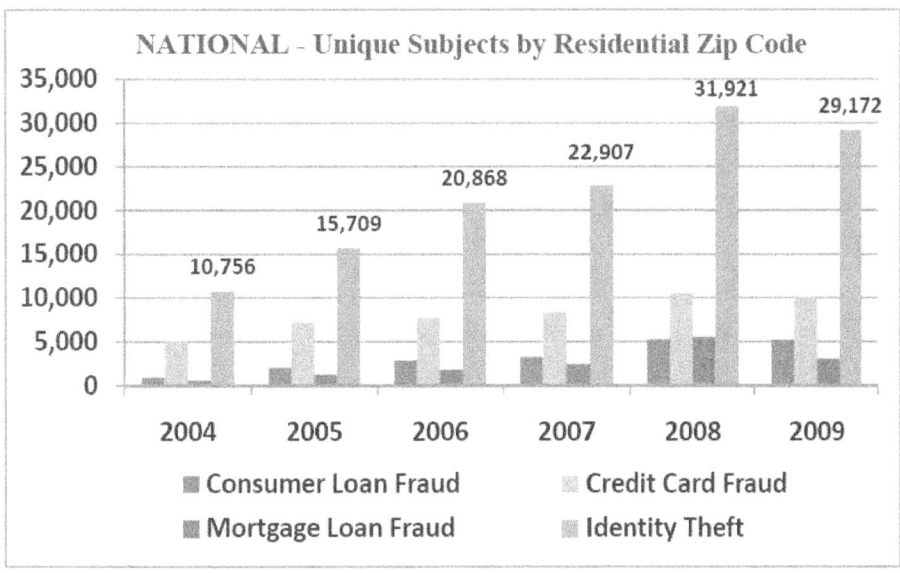

---

24. The number of 2009 unique subjects in this graph is about 3 percent less than that for Map 1. The data used for Map 1 were extensively cleaned while the data for Graph 22 were drawn directly from a statistical summarization, thus explaining the difference.

Means of Theft Discovery

Over 27.5 percent of sample filings reported that identity theft was discovered when customers contacted the filer to question transactions on existing accounts or to contest ownership of recently established accounts, or when customers confirmed identity theft after filers contacted them to question anomalous account transactions. Filers credited their normal account monitoring with uncovering identity theft in nearly 21 percent of sample filings. Searches of commercial databases contributed to discovery of identity theft in 14.5 percent of sample filings, while filer or customer review of customer credit reports was noted as contributing to discovery in 10.5 percent. A federal, state, or local law enforcement agency reportedly brought identity theft to the attention of financial institutions in 5 percent of sample filings. An unexpected call from a bill collector alerted victims to identity theft in 2.5 percent of sample filings. Credit monitoring services or receipt of an unexpected bill were each responsible for uncovering identity theft in less than 2 percent of sample filings.

Methods of Theft Facilitation

The most commonly reported means of identity theft facilitation were actions by friends and family members of the victim. At least 22 percent of sample filings reported mainly family members of the victim, but also friends, as likely complicit in the reported identity theft. The close relationship presumably gave the subject access to the victim's personal information. Also included in this group, though less frequently reported, were others given physical access to the victim's residence, such as caregivers or repair persons. Overall, 27 percent of sample filings reported that the victim knew the person(s) believed to be responsible for the identity theft.

Submission of a fraudulent change of address was a reported means of identity theft facilitation in 4.5 percent of sample filings, as was theft perpetrated by a business insider with access to employee or customer personal information. Spoofing, phishing, and computer hacking were together credited as facilitators in less than 3.5 percent of sample filings. The victim's status as deceased was reported as a facilitator of identity theft in 3 percent of the sample filings. Most of the remaining sample filings reported that the victim had no idea how the identity theft was facilitated.

Several sample filings described the identity thief's use of telephone relay systems intended for use by the deaf to initiate unauthorized banking transactions. The thief may have used this method of communication to avoid the production of a voice print that the bank could create from the tapes it makes of conventional telephone transactions. Several other sample filings described probable money laundering activity in which presumed identity thieves conducted a series of card-to-card transfers using prepaid access cards.

Timing of Discovery, Victim Harm, Abused Accounts, and Mitigation

Timing of Discovery

Graph 24 shows the percentage distribution of time elapsed between last known suspicious activity and discovery of identity theft for sample SAR filings.

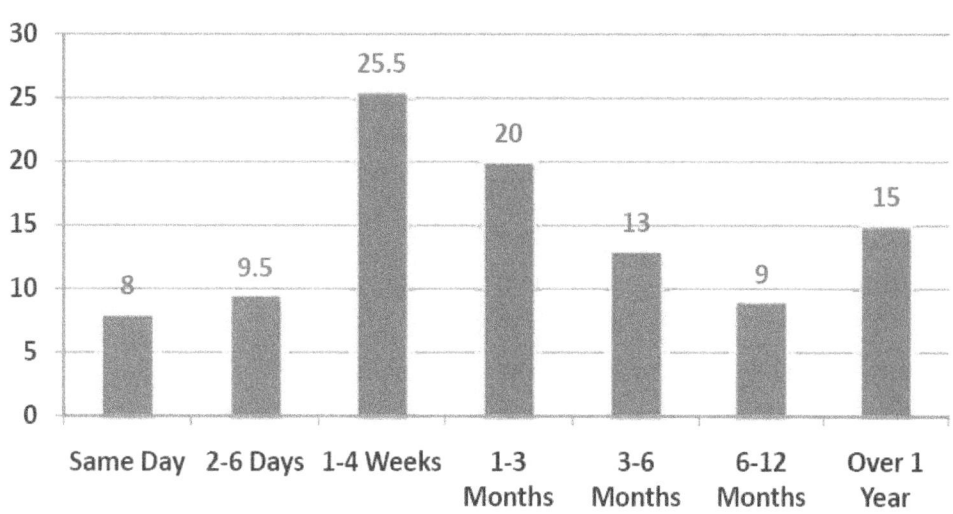

GRAPH 24
Percentage Distribution of Sample SAR Filings Based on Time Elapsed Between Last Identified Suspicious Activity and Discovery

Much of the activity not discovered for an extended period of time involved identity theft perpetrated for the purpose of using the rightful owner's credit history rather than to defraud the victim or a financial institution. Two groups appeared to be motivated to commit identity theft for this reason The first included family members, friends, or acquaintances of victims who had either died or become mentally incapacitated. The second group included individuals unknown to the victim. It is possible that some of these individuals could not establish credit or depository accounts on their own either because of bad credit histories or because of their undocumented status. The unauthorized use of credit, loan, or depository accounts continued for an extended period because the unauthorized users continued to make regular payments on credit or loan accounts, or to use depository accounts, in a non-suspicious manner.

Victim Harm

FinCEN used FTC parameters to measure victim harm. Harm was rated as "low" for victims solely suffering abuse of their existing credit card account(s), "moderate" for victims suffering abuse of other existing financial accounts, and "high" for victims whose identifiers were abused to create new, unauthorized financial accounts of any type.[25]

Victim harm, whether successful or attempted, was assessed as "low" in 10 percent of sample filings, as "moderate" in 11 percent of sample filings, and as "high" in 77 percent of sample filings. However, since 16 percent of sample filings reported unsuccessful attempts to set up unauthorized accounts, actual victim harm was lower at each level.

Abused Accounts

Identity thieves reportedly abused credit card accounts in 45.5 percent of sample filings, loan accounts in 31 percent of sample filings, and depository accounts in 25.5 percent. About 1 percent of sample filings reported the abuse of prepaid cards. Two sample filings reported abuse of auto lease arrangements. Single sample filings reported abuse of an investment account and an Internet payment account.

Mitigation

The most frequently reported actions taken to mitigate successful or attempted illicit activity facilitated by identity theft were account closure (22.5 percent), a filer decision not to complete an account opening or other transaction (19.5 percent), victim filing of an affidavit of forgery (11.5 percent), arrest of the alleged identity thief (5 percent), and shut down of a phishing Web site (1 percent).

---

25. These are the same standards of victim harm that the FTC used in its November 2007 study, *Federal Trade Commission – Identity Theft Survey Report*, prepared by Synovate. http://www.ftc.gov/bcp/edu/microsites/idtheft/. Only the highest level of victim harm reported was recorded for each filing.

Red Flags[26]

Using the language in the Identity Theft Red Flag Reporting Rules jointly published by the U.S. Treasury, FTC, and federal banking agencies, the two most common red flags reported in sample SAR filings were: "The financial institution or creditor is notified by a customer, victim of identity theft, a law enforcement authority, or any other person that it has opened a fraudulent account for a person engaged in identity theft" (nearly 75 percent of relevant sample filings),[27] and "The financial institution or creditor is notified of unauthorized charges or transactions in connection with a customer's covered account" (almost 23 percent of relevant sample filings.)[28]

Other red flags reported included: "Social Security number provided on application is assigned to individual other than the applicant" (8 percent of sample filings),[29] "The Social Security number has not been issued, or is listed on the Social Security Administration's Death Master File" (6 percent of sample filings),[30] "Shortly following the notice of change of address for a covered account, the institution or creditor receives a request for a new, additional, or replacement card or a cell phone, or for the addition of authorized users on the account" (4 percent of sample filings),[31] and "The customer fails to make the first payment or makes an initial payment but no subsequent payments" (4 percent of sample filings).[32]

---

26. Many filings reported multiple red flags.
27. Red flag 26 enumerated in 16 CFR Part 681 Supplement A to Appendix A.
28. Red flag 25 enumerated in 16 CFR Part 681 Supplement A to Appendix A.
29. Red flag derived by analysts during this study.
30. Red flag 10b enumerated in 16 CFR Part 681 Supplement A to Appendix A.
31. Red flag 19 enumerated in 16 CFR Part 681 Supplement A to Appendix A.
32. Red flag 20b enumerated in 16 CFR Part 681 Supplement A to Appendix A.

Filings of Special Note

Individual filings in the sample describe activities that may reveal specific typologies associated with identity theft and the crimes it facilitates.

- A bank reported that an individual opened credit card accounts in the names of individuals with the same name as the alleged identity thief. The identifying information was reportedly provided by an associate of the subject who had access to an employer's loan customer database.

- A bank reported that a person employed as the bookkeeper for a business customer opened an unauthorized business credit card in the name of the business, listing the business's owner as the guarantor. The card was kept current through payments made from the company's business account.

- A filer reported that its former employee allegedly traded employee identifying information to identity thieves in exchange for narcotics.

- A bank reported that an auto dealership employee allegedly used dealership customer identifying information to forge an application for an auto loan to purchase a vehicle on which a customer had already secured a legitimate loan. When the loan funded, the employee allegedly stole the proceeds.

- A bank reported that an employee working in its credit card operations unit had been implicated in a multi-year, million-dollar fraud that benefited the employee's family members and friends. In some intances, the alleged thieves used stolen identifiers to set up unauthorized credit card accounts.

- Several filers reported the deposit of large sums to prepaid cards intended solely to receive ACH credits. Filers determined that the source of funds was either the U.S. Treasury or a state revenue office. Further filer investigation revealed that the purchaser of the prepaid cards had allegedly used stolen identifying information to file fraudulent tax returns claiming multi-thousand dollar refunds. The refunds were routed electronically to the prepaid cards.

- A bank reported that a customer was receiving multiple ACH credits from tax refund anticipation loan companies for the benefit of multiple individuals other than the account holder. Though not specifically suggested by the filer, the subject may have filed false tax returns, claiming refunds using the identifiers of identity theft victims and received the proceeds of refund anticipation loans made on the basis of these false tax refund filings.

- Two filings reported the setup of fraudulent mortgage brokers, which allegedly used identity data gathered from would-be borrowers to originate fraudulent mortgage loans without the knowledge or consent of the named borrowers.

- A bank reported the takeover of a customer's home equity line of credit account and the attempted clearing of a sizeable check against the account. The bank reported that the victim told a bank employee that the victim had been contacted by her family doctor asking for verification of the need to rush a copy of her medical file to a doctor located in the same state as the presumed identity thief. This may suggest that the identity thief was also intending to abuse the victim's medical benefits.

- A bank issuer of credit cards intended to be used to purchase medical services reported a fraudster who posed as multiple genuine healthcare providers using the providers' legitimate license numbers and other identifiers. The subject also used multiple sets of stolen individual identifiers to open multiple credit accounts, and charged the cards for services purportedly provided by the various healthcare providers. The fraudster received payments from the issuing bank following his submission of these fraudulent charges.

- A bank reported that it determined that a customer's depository account had been used by alleged identity thieves as a passthrough account to accumulate funds stolen from corporations. The money was then transferred to foreign accounts. The account was used without the customer's knowledge and accessed with information collected when the customer responded to a phishing email.

- An issuer of prepaid access cards reported receipt of multiple ACH credits to customer prepaid access cards. The credits were payable to third parties unrelated to the cardholders and drawn from online payment accounts. Further, the issuer reported subsequent card-to-card transfers, with all monies eventually transferred to the same depository account. The filer determined that the ACH debits were unauthorized. The filer suggested that the ACH debits were being collected on prepaid access cards held by unwitting participants in an Internet work scam. Proceeds were subsequently transferred to the fraudster's bank account net of "commissions" retained by the unwitting participants.

- A bank reported that a credit card account was taken over and the mailing adress on the account fraudulently changed. The alleged identity thief proceeded to charge nearly $100,000 in less than 2 years, mainly through cash withdrawals. Virtually all of the money was repaid. The legitimate account holder apparently lost track of the account as the bank finally contacted him to inquire about account activity when payments became delinquent. Though not noted by the bank, the circumstances suggested the credit card account takeover may have been effectuated to launder funds, rather than to defraud the card issuer or account holder.

- A credit card issuing bank described a complex money laundering operation reliant upon identity theft. It reported that taken over credit card accounts were used to purchase gift cards at a major chain home improvement store. The gift cards were used to purchase large appliances that were eventually resold in independent (non-chain) appliance stores.

- A filer that makes student loans reported the operation of a student loan fraud ring that it had tied to dozens of fraudulent loans totaling several million dollars. The filer determined that all victims listed on the student loan applications had purchased vehicles at the same auto dealership.

- A filer that makes student loans reported that a fraudster made aggressive attempts to have fraudulent student loans approved by posing as both a university certifier of enrollment and as a fraud investigator.

- Several filings reported that alleged identity thieves set up fraudulent merchant accounts used to charge lost, stolen, or blocked credit card numbers for non-existent merchandise or services. In some instances where cards were blocked, the perpetrator attempted to force charge the transactions.[33]

- A bank reported that a fraudster rented office space and impersonated an actual executive of an existing legitimate company. Bank officials met with the fraudster and granted a large line of credit, which the fraudster subsequently drained and transferred to accounts in another country.

---

33. Force charging occurs when a merchant does not obtain an approval code from the authorization system for the credit card, but rather manually enters the credit card number and a random approval code. Merchants often receive immediate credit in their designated bank account for these charges, which affords the identity thief a window of opportunity to complete the transaction before the charge is reversed as a result of the reconciliation process or complaints lodged by the legitimate credit card owner.

- A bank reported that it had determined that a customer had opened dozens of individual and corporate checking accounts using sets of legitimate identifiers. The bank determined that the actual owners of the identifying information conspired to use the accounts to cash fraudulent and counterfeit items, and then claim to be victims of identity theft, thus defrauding the filer, which the conspirators expected to write off the associated account losses.

- A bank reported that an individual befriended multiple bank customers who lacked basic English skills and offered to help them with their banking activities. The individual then used the bank customers' identifying information to apply for unsecured loans.

NEXT STEPS

The continued annual reporting levels of identity theft filings support the findings of other identity theft studies using different methodologies that identity theft is a significant and growing burden upon the nation's economy. A Javelin Strategy and Research study found that 11.1 million Americans were victims of identity theft in 2009, a surge of 12 percent from the previous year, with an estimated $54 billion cost to the U.S. economy.[34] Identity theft also has less quantifiable, but significant, impacts on public trust in financial accounts and payment systems.

FinCEN will continue to monitor BSA filings related to identity theft and expects to issue additional reports on SAR reporting of identity theft by the securities and futures industries, casinos, and money services businesses. In addition, FinCEN plans to use the data and findings reported in this study as a baseline for a future study to determine the effects that the Identity Theft Red Flag rules have had upon identity theft-related SARs filed after the rules took effect on November 1, 2008.

---

34. See http://www.esecurityplanet.com/features/article.php/3864616/Identity-Theft-Cost-Victims-54B-in-2009.htm. Reference in this report to any specific commercial product, service, process, or enterprise, or the use of any commercial product or enterprise, trade, firm, or corporation name is for the information and convenience of the public, and does not constitute endorsement or recommendation by the Financial Crimes Enforcement Network. With respect to materials generated by entities outside of the Financial Crimes Enforcement Network, permission to use these materials, if necessary, must be obtained from the original source. The Financial Crimes Enforcement Network assumes no responsibility for the content or operation of other Web sites.

www.FinCEN.gov